DINOSAUR
INFOSAURUS

GIGANTIC
DINOSAURS

Katie Woolley

WAYLAND

First published in Great Britain in paperback in 2018
by Wayland

Editor: Elise Short
Design: Peter Clayman
Illustrations: Martin Bustamante

ISBN: 978 1 5263 0464 3

10 9 8 7 6 5 4 3 2 1

Wayland, an imprint of
Hachette Children's Group
Part of Hodder and Stoughton
Carmelite House
50 Victoria Embankment
London EC4Y 0DZ

An Hachette UK Company
www.hachette.co.uk
www.hachettechildrens.co.uk

Printed and bound in China

Picture acknowledgements:
All images courtesy of Shutterstock except
br p29: Nobumichi Tamura/Stocktrek Images/Getty
Images; cover image; tr, tl, bl p29: illustrations by
Martin Bustamante

CONTENTS

GENTLE DINOSAURS

When we think of dinosaurs we often think of mean killing machines, but in fact more than half of all dinosaurs were **herbivores**. This means they ate **plants**. Plant-eaters, such as Triceratops, were hunted and eaten by meat-eaters like Tyrannosaurus rex.

Some plant-eaters were so **big** they had to eat the **weight** of a **small car** in plants every day!

Conifers were **everywhere** during the Mesozoic Era. They made up a large part of a plant-eater's **diet**.

Today, there are 12,000 species of **fern**. For every living type of fern, scientists think there are **nine more fossil species**. That's **108,000 species of fern**. No wonder dinosaurs like Stegosaurus [STEG-oh-SORE-us] loved them!

Not all plant-eating dinosaurs had the right kind of **teeth** for chewing their food. Some dinosaurs **swallowed** plant food in **one big gulp**. The **bacteria** in their **stomachs** helped break down their lunch!

Plant-eaters came in all shapes and sizes. **Long-necked** dinosaurs could reach high up into trees to eat tall leaves and branches. **Short-necked** herbivores grazed on low-lying plants.

CHAIN

Tyrannosaurus rex
[tie-RAN-oh-sore-us rex]

Plant-eaters like **Styracosaurus** ate so much that scientists think they wore their **teeth** down very quickly. Many had teeth arranged in groups called **batteries**. Older teeth on top were constantly replaced by **new teeth** underneath.

FOOD

Triceratops
[tri-SERRA-tops]

palm fronds

Styracosaurus
[sty-RAK-oh-sore-us]

TINY AND TALL

There were **different kinds** of plant-eating dinosaurs: some were **big** and some were **small**. Some walked on **two legs** and others got about on **four**. Some swallowed their food whole, while others chewed their lunch!

This spiky beast is a **Gargoyleosaurus**, pronounced **gahr-goy-lee-oh-sore-us**. Its name means gargoyle lizard.

Gargoyleosaurus was quite **small** – only about 4 m long – but could still weigh as much as 900 kg. That's about the weight of **two polar bears**!

Micropachycephalosaurus [mike-row-pak-ee-keff-ah-loh-sore-us] was a small **rabbit-sized** dinosaur that walked on two legs!

Aquilops [ah-QUILL-ops] was a **tiny** plant-eater that was the size of a **small cat**. It weighed **1.6 kg** and was only **60 cm long**.

Camptosaurus was a Jurassic dinosaur that was only about **1 m tall** but it could **stand up** on two legs to reach food higher up. This plant-eater could run away from predators at a **speed** of up to **25 kilometres per hour**. That's as fast as a **wild turkey**!

Pronounced, **KAMP-toe-sore-us**, its name means bent lizard.

Brachiosaurus was one of the largest plant-eaters that ever lived. This giant was **15 m high** - that's **three giraffes** tall - and **30 m long**. Its neck alone was 9 m long!

Pronounced **BRAK-ee-oh-sore-us**, its name means arm lizard.

Nigersaurus [nee-zhayr-sore-us], a plant-eater from the Early Cretaceous period, had as many as **1,000 teeth**! Experts think it may have grown a new set of teeth every 15 days.

GRAZING GIANTS

Sauropods were a group of plant-eating dinosaurs. They were the **longest**, **heaviest** and **tallest** animals to ever walk the Earth. They usually walked slowly on four column-shaped legs.

These dinosaurs are called Camarasaurus, pronounced **KAM-ar-a-sore-us**. The name means chambered lizard.

Sauropods had long necks and tails, small heads and blunt teeth. Because of their size, a sauropod would have had to eat almost all of the time!

Scientists can't be certain if sauropods like **Apatosaurus** [ah-PAT-oh-sore-us] could hold their **giant necks** up high. To be able to **pump blood** all the way up their long necks, the dinosaur's **heart** alone would have had to weigh **4,000 kg**. That's **15 times heavier** than one side of the heart of a **fin whale**!

Sauropods were **tall** and **heavy**! Did these giants have a clever way of lightening their load? **Fossil bones** have been found with small pockets of air, called **air sacs**, inside them. These air sacs might have helped to **lighten** the weight of the skeletons of these big dinosaurs.

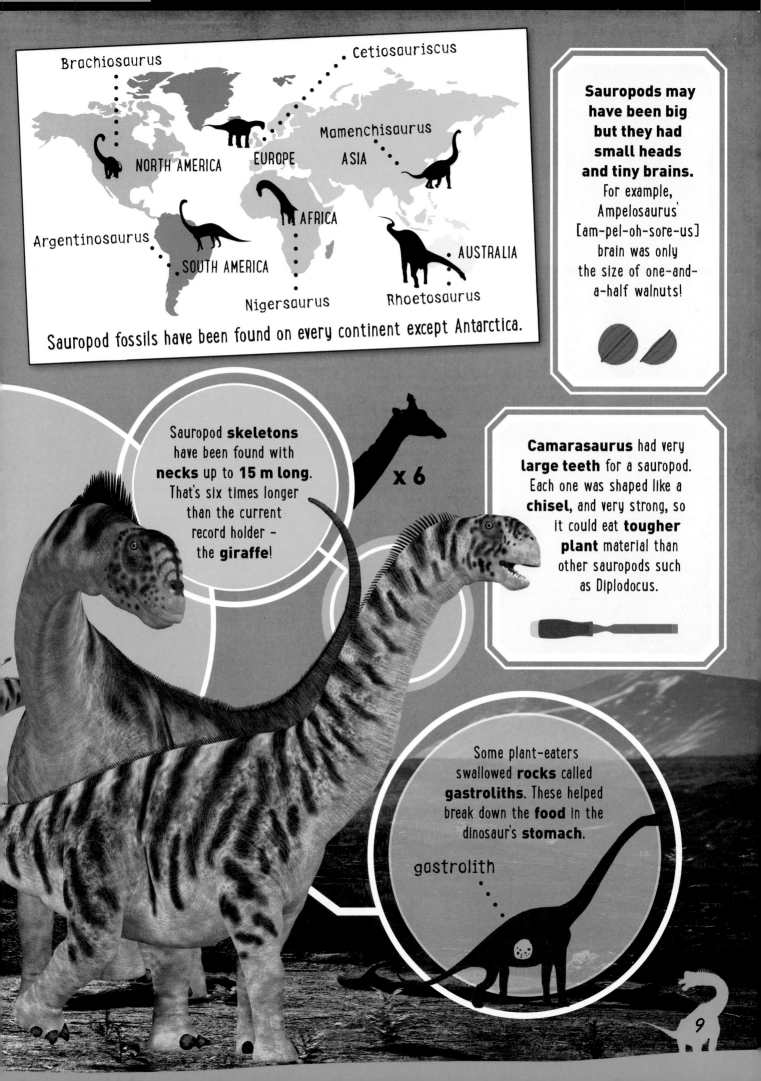

Brachiosaurus

Cetiosauriscus

Mamenchisaurus

NORTH AMERICA

EUROPE

ASIA

Argentinosaurus

AFRICA

AUSTRALIA

SOUTH AMERICA

Nigersaurus

Rhoetosaurus

Sauropod fossils have been found on every continent except Antarctica.

Sauropods may have been big but they had small heads and tiny brains. For example, Ampelosaurus' [am-pel-oh-sore-us] brain was only the size of one-and-a-half walnuts!

Sauropod **skeletons** have been found with **necks** up to **15 m long**. That's six times longer than the current record holder – the **giraffe**!

x 6

Camarasaurus had very **large teeth** for a sauropod. Each one was shaped like a **chisel**, and very strong, so it could eat **tougher plant** material than other sauropods such as Diplodocus.

Some plant-eaters swallowed **rocks** called **gastroliths**. These helped break down the **food** in the dinosaur's **stomach**.

gastrolith

DINO DEFENCE

Plant-eating dinosaurs were always on the look out for **predators**. They didn't want to end up as a meat-eater's lunch! Scientists think plant-eaters had **tough, leathery skin** to **protect** from razor-sharp, meat-eating teeth. Some dinosaurs also had **horns**, **spikes** and **tail clubs** to defend themselves!

Thick-skulled dinosaurs like **Stegoceras** [ste-GOS-er-as] might have used their **heads** to head butt one another during **fights** over a mate!

Ankylosaurus was covered in **bony plates**, called **scutes**, and big spikes. This body armour was similar to an **armadillo's** today.

Pronounced **an-KIE-loh-sore-us**, its name means stiff lizard.

Kentrosaurus had long, bony **spikes** running in pairs down its back and tail for **protection**. It could swing its tail at an attacker with enough force to fracture a human skull!

Pronounced **ken-TROH-sore-us**, its name means spiky lizard.

Centrosaurus' head was built for **defence**. It had a **bony frill** to protect its neck, two **large horns** on top of the frill and a pair of **small horns** over its eyes. It also had a horn on its nose, like a **rhinoceros**.

Pronounced **Cen-TROH-sore-us**, its name means sharp pointed lizard.

Size was often a plant-eating dinosaur's **biggest defence**. Only fierce, hungry **predators** and packs of meat-eating dinosaurs, such as Deinonychus [die-NON-i-kuss], would have dared take on some of these gigantic beasts.

This dinosaur is an **Apatosaurus** pronounced **ah-PAT-oh-sore-us**. Its name means deceptive lizard.

Apatosaurus may have used its long **tail** to **strike** at its enemies.

Apatosaurus wasn't a defenceless plant-eater. Its **height, whip-like tail** and **clawed feet** meant it could have put up quite a **fight** with any of the biggest predators it lived alongside. The predator **Allosaurus** [AL-oh-saw-russ] wouldn't even have been able to reach Apatosaurus' neck during an attack!

SAUROPOD HERDS

Scientists think that some plant-eating dinosaurs lived in **herds** or **family groups**, just like buffalo and zebra do today. Possibly even some of the **largest dinosaurs** to ever walk the Earth – the **sauropods** – lived in groups.

Alamosaurus, pronounced **ah-la-mow-SORE-us**, means Alamo lizard.

Living in herds offered some protection from predators as enormous dinosaurs would have needed to graze continuously throughout the day. Some plant-eaters might have **migrated** large distances in groups in search of **food**, like **elephants** do today.

Fossilised footprints in Texas, USA, might have been made by **23 sauropods**. The different footprint sizes may reveal that the **adults led their young** across land, possibly walking long distances to find food.

A **bone bed** is an area of rock that contains **bones** of fossilised animals. Scientists have found bone beds of **dinosaur bones**. How did they get there? Perhaps these dinosaurs were living in a herd and became **trapped in mud**, caught up in a **flood** or they died because of **droughts** in the area.

Alamosaurus fossil finds suggest that **juvenile** dinosaurs may have **stuck together**. This may have been down to **size**, as they might have had different **dietary needs** from adult dinosaurs. Living together would have given them greater **protection** from predators, too.

The largest sauropods weighed ten times more than an elephant. To see these creatures in a herd would have been quite a sight!

Fossilised trackways reveal where dinosaurs might have walked. Some **herds** could have been made up of **hundreds** of individuals.

13

THE HEAVIEST SAUROPOD

Argentinosaurus was an **enormous sauropod**! It was **35 m long** and weighed in at **70,000 kg**. This giant lived during the **Cretaceous** period.

Argentinosaurus, pronounced **AR-gent-eeno-sore-us**, means Argentina lizard.

Argentinosaurus may have been **preyed** on by the biggest meat-eater of the time – **Giganotosaurus** [gig-an-OH-toe-SORE-us].

Argentinosaurus carried its weight on four huge column-shaped legs.

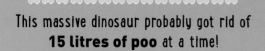

This massive dinosaur probably got rid of **15 litres of poo** at a time!

Argentinosaurus fed on **leaves** at the top of tall trees, using its long **neck** to reach up **high**. It used its teeth for chewing and grinding its food.

Argentinosaurus may have continued to **grow** throughout its **entire life**. It may have taken as long as **40 years** to reach its **adult size**!

Scientists still don't know how this giant held up its **neck**. Its huge **heart** would have had to work very hard to pump blood up its neck to its head when it raised it up to eat!

Argentinosaurus may have lived in **herds** to **protect** its **eggs** and young from predator **attack**.

One Argentinosaurus **vertebra** was about **1.5 m tall**. This is almost the same height as the biggest jump a **red kangaroo** can do!

An Argentinosaurus **egg** was about 20 cm wide – the size of a **basketball**.

Its weight meant Argentinosaurus moved at about **8 kph** – as fast as a **tortoise**.

SAILS AND SPINES

Amargasaurus was a bizarre-looking **Early Cretaceous** dinosaur that, at **12 m long**, was the length of one-and-a-half buses. Amargasaurus had two rows of **spines** that may have joined together to form a **sail** running down the length of its back.

Amargasaurus, pronounced **A-MARG-oh-sore-us**, means Amarga lizard.

These dinosaurs laid between **6 and 12 eggs** in a cluster. Each egg was **15 cm wide**!

Amargasaurus had curved **claws** on each back foot. Could they have been used for **digging**?

Scientists aren't sure what the **sail** on its back was for but it might have been for **protection** or to **attract a mate**.

The **sail** might also have been used to **control** Amargasaurus' body **temperature** – absorbing warmth from the sun if it was cold, and helping release heat if it got too hot.

This herbivore ate **tough plants**, such as **ferns** and **conifers**, using its **blunt teeth** to strip leaves from branches.

It's rare to find **skulls** of sauropods but in 2014 scientists were able to study an Amargasaurus skull. It showed that this dinosaur had short inner **ears**. This means it might not have been able to hear as well as some other sauropods.

This plant-eater is smaller than many other sauropods. Yet, it still weighed **9,000 kg** – about the same as **six hippos**.

DOUBLE BEAM GIANT

Diplodocus lived during the **Late Jurassic** period and is one of the **longest** animals that ever roamed the Earth.

Pronounced **DIP-low DOCK-us**, its name means double beam.

Diplodocus' **tail** was long and strong, and may have been used as a **balance**, allowing it to rear up on its back legs to reach food that was very high up.

Diplodocus had a **long tail** that might have been used as a **whip** during a predator **attack**. The tail weighed **1,590 kg** so would have sounded as loud as cannon fire!

Diplodocus **poo** would have dropped from a great height. On the ground it may have formed a pool about **10 m wide** – yuck!

For a dinosaur as big as Diplodocus, its **eggs** were quite **small** – only 1.5 kg. Scientists think this made the eggs in the nest vulnerable to fewer predators as they were able to **hatch** into baby dinosaurs more **quickly**.

Diplodocus weighed up to 25,000 kg – as much as a full concrete mixer!

At 26 m long Diplodocus was the same length as three buses!

This dinosaur's **neck** and tail was made up of almost **100 vertebrae**.

Diplodocus lived at the same time as some of the fiercest meat-eating dinosaurs, like Allosaurus and Ceratosaurus [Keh-RAT-oh-sore-us]. Luckily, Diplodocus' **giant size** probably meant it was **safe** from most **predators**.

This giant plant-eater had rows of **teeth** like a **comb** that it used to strip the leaves from plants and swallow whole.

Diplodocus probably didn't **sleep** for any long periods of time. It's thought it **constantly ate, walked** and **slept** throughout the day and night.

BONES AND PLATES

Stegosaurus was a **large**, slow-moving plant-eater. It had **17 bony plates** on its back, buried within its skin, which might have helped keep the dinosaur **cool**. The plates might have **protected** the dinosaur from **predator attack** or even been used in **mating displays**. Scientists aren't sure!

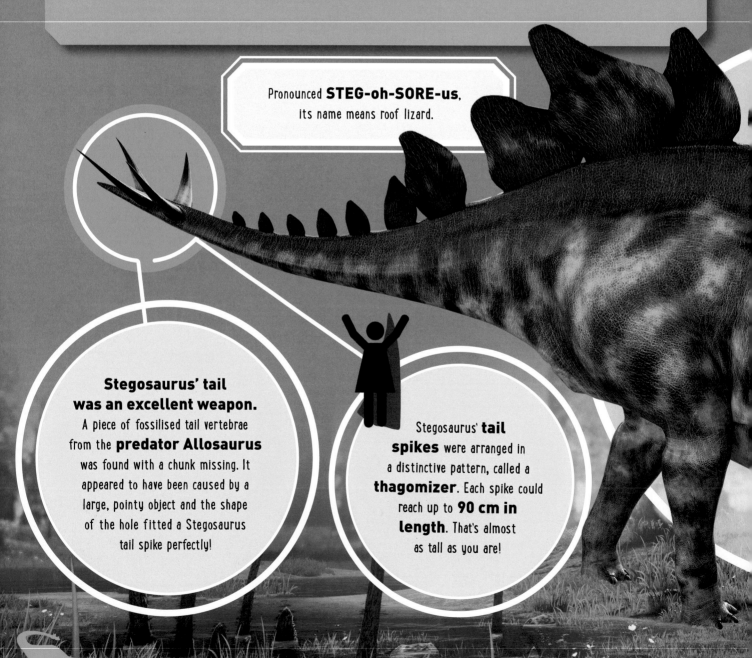

Pronounced **STEG-oh-SORE-us**, its name means roof lizard.

Stegosaurus' tail was an excellent weapon. A piece of fossilised tail vertebrae from the **predator Allosaurus** was found with a chunk missing. It appeared to have been caused by a large, pointy object and the shape of the hole fitted a Stegosaurus tail spike perfectly!

Stegosaurus' **tail spikes** were arranged in a distinctive pattern, called a **thagomizer**. Each spike could reach up to **90 cm in length**. That's almost as tall as you are!

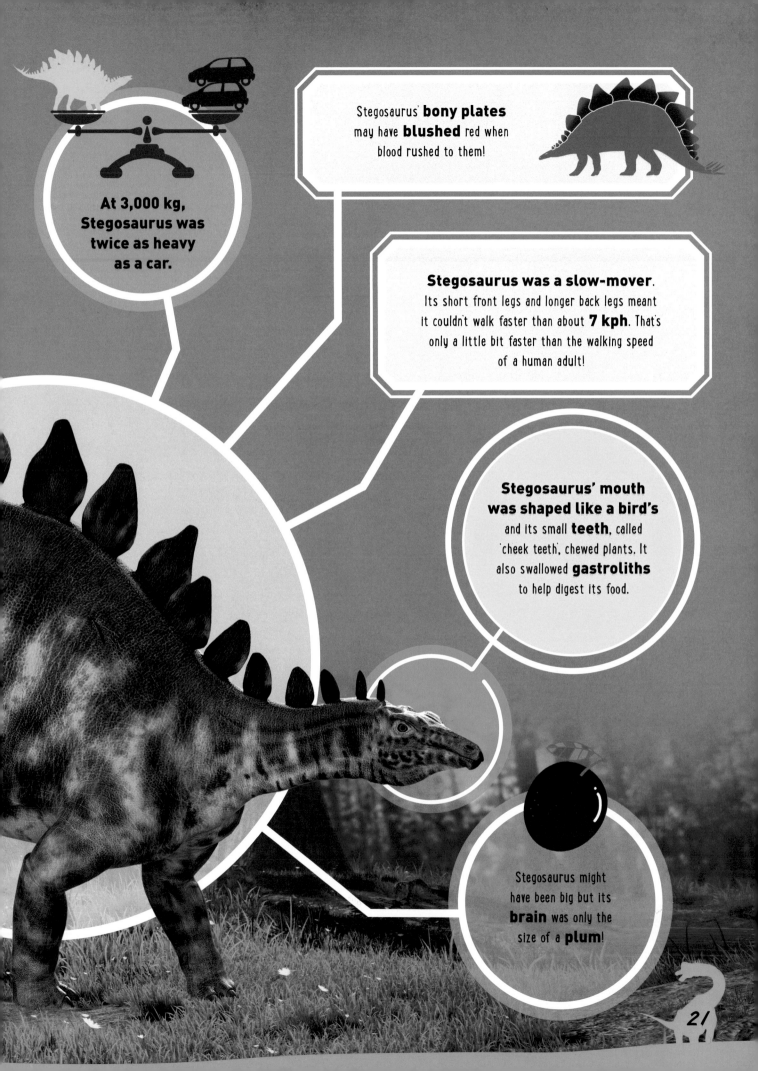

At 3,000 kg, Stegosaurus was twice as heavy as a car.

Stegosaurus' **bony plates** may have **blushed** red when blood rushed to them!

Stegosaurus was a slow-mover. Its short front legs and longer back legs meant it couldn't walk faster than about **7 kph**. That's only a little bit faster than the walking speed of a human adult!

Stegosaurus' mouth was shaped like a bird's and its small **teeth**, called 'cheek teeth', chewed plants. It also swallowed **gastroliths** to help digest its food.

Stegosaurus might have been big but its **brain** was only the size of a **plum!**

THREE-HORNED HEAD

One of the most famous dinosaurs is Triceratops. This plant-eater, with its **three horns**, parrot-like **beak** and large **frill**, is one of the largest and most striking dinosaurs to have ever lived.

Triceratops **bones** have been found in the **fossilised poo** of Tyrannosaurus rex. **T. Rex** probably ate Triceratops for lunch!

Pronounced **tri-SERRA-tops**, its name means three-horned face.

Triceratops might have **charged** when threatened, just like a **rhino** charges today.

When Triceratops **fossils** were first discovered in 1887, they were mistaken for **bison bones**. It took a year for experts to notice the mistake.

A baby Triceratops' **head** was about the same size as a human head. But palaeontologists have discovered adult Triceratops **skulls** that are over 2 m long!

Triceratops' **frill** may have **flushed** red or pink because it had lots of blood vessels in it. This might have been a way to **signal** to others in a **herd** or to **attract a mate**.

Triceratops ate low-lying plants and shrubs – and a lot of them every day! This meant it needed lots of **teeth**. Triceratops got through between **400** and **800 teeth** in its lifetime!

Triceratops was built for defence. Its enormous **frill** acted as a **shield** to protect its soft body from **attack**. And the 2-m-long **horns** on its head were long enough to pierce the heart of Tyrannosaurus rex! They might have also been used in **mating displays**, like **deer antlers** today.

The small **horn** on its snout was made from **keratin**, the same material as fingernails.

Triceratops lived right up until the end of the dinosaurs, about 65 million years ago.

SUIT OF ARMOUR

Ankylosaurus was a plant-eater that was **protected** from head to toe with **bony plates** and **spikes**. It was almost as wide as it was long. A meat-eater would have had to be really hungry to attack this amoured dinosaur!

Ankylosaurus' **tail club** was made of **fused bone.** This is when the bones are joined together to form one big mass of bone. The tail club was so strong it could **shatter bone** during a fight.

Ankylosaurus didn't chew its food. Breaking down all that food in its **stomach** might have made this dinosaur very **gassy**!

Ankylosaurus' size meant that it ate a lot every day! It would strip the leaves from branches as it moved slowly through its habitat at about **10 kph**. That's the same speed as a king penguin waddling!

This plant-eater weighed as much as 7,000 kg - that's about twice the weight of a **killer whale**!

Ankylosaurus was about 7 m long. That's about the same length as three-and-a-half beds.

The **spikes** on its head may have been strong enough to **break** a predator's **teeth**.

Pronounced **an-KIE-loh-sore-us**, its name means stiff lizard.

CLAWED CREATURE

Iguanodon was a plant-eating dinosaur that lived during the **Early Cretaceous** period. It was first discovered in **Sussex**, **UK** in 1822 by Mary and Gideon Mantell. Fossils have since been found in other parts of **Europe**, **Africa** and **North America**.

Scientists have found several **fossils** from different Iguanodons together in the same place. This could mean these dinosaurs **lived in groups for protection**.

Iguanodon moved at 24 kph. That's the same speed as a charging bull!

Pronounced **ig-WHA-noh-don**, its name means 'iguana tooth' because Mary Mantell thought its teeth looked like those of an **iguana**.

When Iguanodon was first **discovered**, some scientists didn't think the bones belonged to a dinosaur. They were dismissed as **fish teeth** or the teeth of a **rhinoceros**!

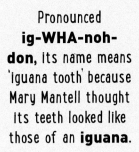

This dinosaur could walk on four or two legs – whatever it fancied!

Iguanodon had large **thumb claws** for **self-defence** and **flexible fingers**, possibly for **foraging** for food.

Iguanodon had **three short, thick toes** on its back feet. These might have been **padded** to allow this huge dinosaur to evenly spread its weight across its feet and walk more comfortably.

This plant-eater may have had **bendy fingers** to hold its food and possibly break open seeds and fruit.

MORE DINO FACTS

Plant-eating dinosaurs were some of the strangest creatures to ever walk the Earth. Check out these fascinating dino facts!

PARASAUROLOPHUS

HEIGHT: 2.8 m

LENGTH: 11 m

WEIGHT: 3,500 kg

LIVED: Late Cretaceous

LOCATION: Canada, USA

FIRST FOSSIL DISCOVERY: Alberta, Canada 1922

FACT: Parasaurolophus may have used its curved crest to make a noise to warn other members of its herd of danger.

GALLIMIMUS

HEIGHT: 1.9 m

LENGTH: 6 m

WEIGHT: 200 kg

LIVED: Late Cretaceous

LOCATION: Mongolia

FIRST FOSSIL DISCOVERY: Gobi Desert, Mongolia, 1972

FACT: Gallimimus was one of the fastest dinosaurs. At 70 kph, it could run as fast as an ostrich!

LESOTHOSAURUS

HEIGHT: 0.5 m
LENGTH: 1 m
WEIGHT: 10 kg
LIVED: Late Jurassic
LOCATION: Lesotho
FIRST FOSSIL DISCOVERY: Lesotho, 1978
FACT: This early dinosaur had five-fingered hands!

NOTHRONYCHUS

HEIGHT: Unknown
LENGTH: 5.3 m
WEIGHT: 900 kg
LIVED: Late Cretaceous
LOCATION: USA
FIRST FOSSIL DISCOVERY: New Mexico, USA, 2001
FACT: This strange dinosaur may have evolved from a meat-eater to a plant-eater.

STYGIMOLOCH

HEIGHT: 1.3 m
LENGTH: 3 m
WEIGHT: 200 kg
LIVED: Late Cretaceous
LOCATION: USA
FIRST FOSSIL DISCOVERY: First discovered in the 1800s. Named in 1983, Montana, USA
FACT: Stygimoloch had a ring of horns around its skull. Some people think it looks a bit demonic!

MINMI

HEIGHT: 0.9 m
LENGTH: 3 m
WEIGHT: 50 kg
LIVED: Early Cretaceous
LOCATION: Australia
FIRST FOSSIL DISCOVERY: Coast Island, Australia, 1964
FACT: This dinosaur was named after Minmi Crossing in Queensland, Australia.

GLOSSARY

acid a chemical in the stomach that helps break down food

bacteria tiny living things. Some kinds of bacteria live in the digestive system and help break down food

bone bed an area of rock that contains bones of fossilised animals

conifer a kind of tree

Cretaceous period a period in Earth's history, between 144 and 65 million years ago

dietary of or relating to a diet or to the rules of diet

digestion the process of breaking down food

drought a long period without water. Animals, plants and people need water to survive.

fern a flowerless plant

food chain group of living things (animals and plants) where each member of the group is eaten in turn by another

foraging search for food

fossil the remains of an animal or plant, preserved for millions of years

frill a fringe of feathers, hair or bone around the neck of an animal

gastrolith a small stone swallowed by some animals to aid digestion

herbivore an animal that eats plants

Jurassic period a period of Earth's history, between 206 and 144 million years ago

juvenile a young or baby animal

Mesozoic Era a period of time in Earth's history

migrate to travel from one area to another in search of food or due to the seasons

nutrient a substance that provides nourishment to the body

palaeontologist a scientist who studies fossils

predator an animal that eats other animals

sauropods a group of dinosaurs that walked on four legs, had long tails and necks, small heads and thick, column-shaped limbs

scute a thick bony plate on the back of an animal

species a group of closely-related animals that are very similar

trackway a beaten or trodden path. A fossilised trackway is one that has been preserved for millions of years.

Triassic period a period in Earth's history, between 248 and 206 million years ago

vertebrae the bones that make up the spine of an animal

FURTHER INFORMATION

Further Reading

Planet Earth: Birth of the Dinosaurs by Michael Bright (Wayland, 2016)

Atlas of Dinosaurs by Emily Hawkins and Lucy Letherland (Wide-Eyed Editions, 2017)

Eyewitness: Dinosaurs (DK Children, 2014)

History VIPs: Mary Anning by Kay Barnham (Wayland, 2016)

Websites

www.natgeokids.com/uk/discover/animals/prehistoric-animals/meet-some-deadly-dinos/

www.dkfindout.com/uk/dinosaurs-and-prehistoric-life/dinosaurs/

www.bbc.co.uk/nature/life/Dinosaur

www.nhm.ac.uk/discover/dino-directory/index.html

INDEX